Firescreen of yaffles and greater spotted
woodpeckers described on page 123.

By the same author:
THE PEACOCK VANE COOKERY BOOK:
RECIPES to RELISH (2nd & 3rd impression PELHAM BOOKS)

THE GLORY of the GARDEN
& The Cycle of the Year

First published in Great Britain by Peacock Vane Bonchurch
Isle of Wight
Copyright © Joan Wolfenden 1983

ISBN 0 9506749 2 3

Produced by CROSS PRINT, NEWPORT. Isle of Wight
Printed in Singapore.

For dearest Alice, the perfect aunt,
counsellor and friend ~

BIBLIOGRAPHY.

History of Folk Cross Stitch   Heinz Edgar Kiewe   Sebaldus-Verlag Nuremberg.

Charted Peasant Designs from Saxon Transylvania   Heinz Edgar Kiewe   Dover Publications Inc. New York.

The Land of Nursery Rhyme   Alice Daglish & Ernest Rhys (1931) J. M. Dent & Sons Ltd.

Patchwork Quilts Averil Colby (1965) Botsford. 4 Fitzhardinge St, Portman Square London W.1.

Patchwork.   Averil Colby (1958) B.T. Batsford Ltd.

50 Canvas Embroidery Stitches.   Coats Sewing Group.

Church Kneelers   J and P. Coats Ltd. (1972)

Catalogue of English Domestic Embroidery   John L Nevinson (1938) Victoria and Albert Museum.

Then the eyes of both of them were opened and they discovered that they were naked; so they stitched fig-leaves together and made themselves loincloths.

Genesis III verse 7

THE SATISFACTION
OF STITCHERY

JOAN WOLFENDEN · · ·

Handwritten by the author
and illustrated with her work
Photography Bill Holden··

INTRODUCTION

Peacock Vane is a regency house near the sea in the south of the Isle of Wight. It has been run for more than quarter of a century by my family and me. I have always enjoyed cooking, gardening and needlework. When we decided, after the war, to try a new way of life the cooking was a vital part of the hotel and the restaurant. As the years went by customers kept on saying: "When are you going to write your cookery book?" and eventually I got it written down and illustrated and we called it: Recipes to Relish.

Then I handed Peacock Vane over to my son John and to Rosalind, his delightful wife, and "retired." This gave me time to take seriously to gardening. Eventually after a new question of: "When are you going to write your gardening book?" I wrote and illustrated: The Glory of the Garden.

Now the time has come to put the five sections of the Satisfaction of Stitchery to-gether. When customers were reluctant to go to bed and I had to stay up too, I survived because I always had a piece of patchwork, embroidery, collage or canvas work in my hands. This is why I never worked on a frame. Just working was cranky enough! So I used or devised methods of keeping the material straight and true.

The text begins with simple cross stitch from the samplers which make the title pages and the end papers. This flows into the section on Canvas Embroidery, followed by simple Patchwork. Collage is more difficult; ~ finally the joys of Traditional Embroidery are discussed.

It took a long time to find a suitable text from the Bible ~ old samplers always had an improving text ~~ It had been better if I had started at the beginning instead of working backwards! But I did find the first recorded allusion to needlework.

Thirty years of needlecraft is the basis of the illustrations. Stitchery can be very soothing and also satisfying. There is a feeling of love and happiness where a certain amount of handwork is used to garnish our homes.

Yaffles,
Bonchurch.

17th July 1982 ~ April 1983

ACKNOWLEDGEMENTS
and THANKS for help to:

Ventnor Library, particularly from Ian Snow
The Isle of Wight County Council and for kind permission
Heinz Edgar Kiewe for designs from his History of Folk Cross Stitch to use their Coat of Arms
and 6 Charted Peasant Designs from Saxon Transylvania.
J. M. Dent for kind permission to use Charles Folkard's designs.
Margaret Rule for the design of the Roman mosaic at Chichester
Tom Bryan for his generosity with preliminary photography
and for Jacob's Sheep (p. 113)

The men and women of the Parish of Bonchurch
and other friends who joined in the embroidery for our church,
the patchwork carpet and with fundraising for the materials used:
Alfred & Janet Tedman, Alan & Ruby Thom-son, Gwen & Ron Newnham,
Kath & Norah Johnston, Elinor & Henry Cleaver, Mary Day, Betty
McKinley, Joy Smith, Guy Gluckstein, Gayna Illovy, Joyce Thompson,
Fidi & Gaby Warner, Lydia Lovegrove, Ivy and Betty Lowe, Vi Wells,
Joan & Jane Brett, Joan Baker, Leslie Russell, Jack & Marjorie
Payne, Phyl Brett, Thelma & Russell Groves, Betty & Norman
Maslen, Christine & David Brown, Julia Keeley,
Rosemary Whitehead and Nora Beach.
Also to: Sally & Bob Garratt, Jim & Kathy Hayles,
David & Gunda Duggan, Mike & Joan Souter, Verna
Quinnell, Patric & Lizzie Hosier, Peter & Sibyl White,
Richard, Hazel & Russell Sparks and all my family
especially Venetia. Finally and most gratefully to
Joyce Carew for proof reading.

If I've forgotten any one please feel included and
accept both my thanks and apologies.

The author at her work ~~

9

CONTENTS

COLOURED PAGES

The title page and dust jacket are made as

a cross stitch sampler.   To make a sampler is very
easy but it is time consuming.   Children and beginners are often put off by starting on an over ambitious
piece of work.   Why not begin with a simple table
mat or a tray cloth?   Cross stitch is easy.   It
is worked on evenweave linen or wool which can be
bought at good needlework shops.   I chose the wool
because there are 18 threads to the inch.   I find this
less taxing on my eyes.

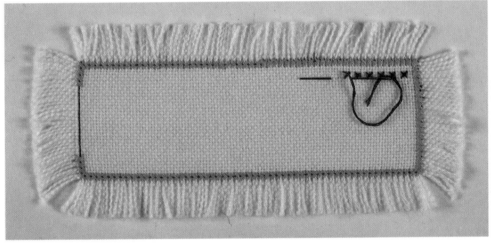

.   For a table mat, having decided the size,
it is a great protection to the work if one row
of machine stitching is placed carefully on the
threads about 3/4" from the edge.   Then, if the
machining is in the right place, a row of cross
stitch can be worked to hide it.   When the
mat is finished the outer edges can be frayed to
make an attractive edging.   I have used a
dark machine stitching to make it show up

13

Obviously you would use the same colour as the background.
The continuous row of cross stitch is a great help later
on as it makes it easier to count the threads to work out
a design.   It is simpler to count cross stitches than to
count threads which tend to distract the eye and lead
to confusion.

The stitches are worked from right to left. The
needle is put in on the lower row and taken over
two threads diagonally. The second stitch is again
from right to left across the top two threads. The
third stitch returns the thread to the bottom row
diagonally. The needle is then brought out along
the lower row ready for the next cross to be made in
the same way. I hope the diagram makes this
clear.

The top row shows the
stitches separately. The
cross on the right of the 2nd
row is one finished cross
stitch. The final group is
a continuous row of cross stitch.

Many charming traditional designs exist
of birds, flowers, leaves and geometric patterns.   Traditionally patterns were worked
in red and black. For the table mat it is a good
plan to choose two shades out of your dinner
service. After strengthening the edge and working one continuous row of crosses a simple design

can be worked with a floral motif, or a geometric pattern to complete the mat. Simplicity always looks best.

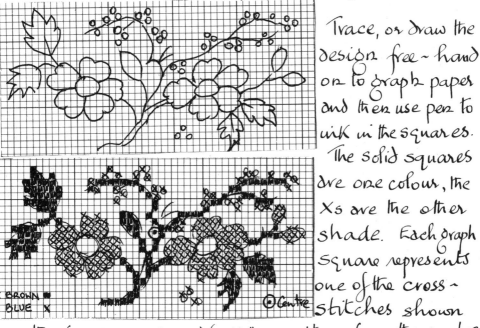

Trace, or draw the design free-hand on to graph paper and then use pen to ink in the squares. The solid squares are one colour, the Xs are the other shade. Each graph square represents one of the cross-stitches shown on the facing page. Work the pattern from the centre.

Breaking with tradition in the title pages I have used the four colours; olive green, old gold, orange and dark brown. But I have never used more than two colours in the individual designs except for the logo S of C where I have combined all four.

The history of Folk-Cross Stitch by Heinz Edgar Kiewe is my bible for this type of work. This excellent book is full of designs and useful, interesting advice. It is fun to work out one's own design interlaced with historic stitches. It is most satisfying because the end product is then unique.

I work these cross stitch patterns in six stranded cotton, using 2 strands at a time. Choose two, or at most three or four shades. I have taken the blue & brown shades from the bone china ware Known as: Old Colony made by Royal Doulton.

If you enjoy making a simple set of table mats then something more ambitious may be tackled. I have a personal rule. Never do I allow myself to start on a second piece of work before the first one is finished. This is a tremendous spur to getting the first one out of the way. While I am finishing pedestrian work my mind is set free to design and work out the next project.

CANVAS EMBROIDERY.

The simple cross stitches can be worked just as well on canvas. Canvas embroidery, often wrongly referred to as tapestry is the next stage in satisfying stitches. With canvas we fill in all the background with coloured thread ~ usually wool. I always use Appletons ~ the colours are beautiful, the texture supreme and the quality perfect. Either crewel wool or so called tapestry wool may be selected. Start on the tapestry wool but the minute you feel competent go on to the crewel wool. This can be used, like the stranded wool in one, two, three, four, five or six strands. Most beginners start using tent stitch ~ This is like the first stitch of cross stitch but always the needle travels further at the back of the work giving a good texture. However if worked out of a frame it can be disastrous as the work can be pulled right out of shape.

Come up at 1. Go down at 2. Come up at 3 and so on. The same look can be obtained on the front of the canvas but a basket weave will result on the back of the canvas if the diagonal method is used. Ascending the diagonal the needle is held horizontally. Descending the

18

needle is held vertically. Start at the top right hand corner and work up and down. The numbers are intended to be helpful. Come up at 1 and go down at 2. Up at 3 and down at 4. When the top is reached at 26 come up at 27 and go down at 28, up at 29, down at 30 and so on. The stitch sounds daunting but after a bit of trial and error on a spare oddment of canvas will soon be vanquished and once tamed is very easy!

The secret is to fill the canvas holes with the wool so that a good firm piece of work is made which will last forever. Don't pull tight. The wool should lie comfortably on the canvas. Work done with love that takes many hours to complete should be for posterity ~ not the rag bag or a cupboard full of "unfinished symphonies".

One of the most ambitious pieces of work I have ever undertaken is the wall hanging at the back of our village church: St. Boniface. I was inspired by the Isle of Wight coat of Arms to write a poem: All this Beauty is of God. Then I worked the wall hanging of the Four Seasons ~ measuring six foot by three foot. It tells of the four guardian angels of the seasons. Spring is a youth, Summer he's in his

19

prime, Autumn ageing and Winter bald headed
and old. Their wings are white tinged with
the colours of the season and are worked in
florentine stitch. The wings form archways
framing our view of St. Boniface Down, the
highest point of the Island, and the ever-
changing sea. The angels' faces are obscured
by their wings.

NG · THERE · IS · A · SEASON ·

Winter was worked first. Four pieces of
canvas were used else the work would have been
cumbersome. Later they were joined together
and the joins embroidered. The hanging was
started in the Winter as it is easier to get the
colours right if working at the same time of
the year. Winter, the season of rest, shows

many things asleep beneath the good earth. Hedgehog, worms, corms, bulbs and fleshy roots. The hazel has dormant catkins and the wild rose still holds its red, shiny hips. Iris stylosa is in flower.

In Spring the snowdrop appears above its bulb, crocus above its corm and likewise daffodils. Hedgehog is just awakening. The catkins are blowing in the breeze ~ the grey skies of Winter have turned to a Spring blue. Different canvas embroidery stitches are used to give texture and definition to the design. I was sitting in the Entrance Hall at Peacock Vane working on one of the panels ~ when a young girl and her mother passed by. The girl said that she was learning tapestry at school and she had been taught that all the stitches had to go the same way! A profound truth but she thought that there was only one stitch: tent.

It is a pity beginners are nearly always taught this stitch. It is the most inclined to pull the canvas out of shape. That is why I recommend diagonal stitch (p. 18). Also, of course, the girl made the usual mistake. Real tapestry is woven, not embroidered.

The Autumn panel shows the ripeness of the harvest. Hazel nuts are plump and passion flowers are become orange fruits. The berries of the cuckoo pint stand now as a glowing spike: Lords and Ladies.

In the Summer country folk call the wild arum:
Jack in his Pulpit ~ apt ~ and that is why it is
included.   I always try to get a woodpecker (yaffle)
or a peacock somewhere in my designs. The
Autumn panel shows a peacock butterfly on
the buddleia.   Passion flower is included both
for its religious significance and for the pure
beauty of its flowers and fruits.   Hedgehog
is there, too, marching proudly with his three
hedge piglets.
   Many different stitches are used to give both
depth and texture to the work.   The striped effect
of the sky is inspired by a Chinese technique.
   Mike Adams, an artist who lives in the
Seychelles, paints his water colours in this way
and I thought I would use his style. It was he
who told me that he had copied the Chinese.
The stitch used I call George and Andrew ~
because it is the saltire covered by an upright
cross worked over nine holes.

Work from right to left.
Come up at 1. Go down at
2. Come up at 3. Go
down at 4. Come up at
5. Go down at 6. Come
up at 7. Go down at 8.
From 8 take the thread on
the back over to 9. Come up and start over again
into 3.

saltire
St George's cross.

		3	8	2
G	E	O	R	G	E	&			5		6
A	N	D	R	E	W			9		1	7	4

23

ALL THIS BEAUTY IS OF GOD

In praise of Winter when the sky is grey:
Hips glow, jasmine gleams and from seeming tussocks
                                    of grass
The brave Iris finds itself a path.
Velvet the colours of the sky ~ Crisp with laser beams of sun
Causing the leaves to shine.
Underneath the earth, peacefully asleep,
lie hedgehog, bulb, corm and root ~
Waiting the call of Spring, the golden herald:
Hear the trumpets of the daffodils!
Mark their loud shout: "Rouse up you lie-a-beds!"
"Make haste! Saprise! Buds swell!
Be about your mating and your growing."
Glory be to Summer and the Autumn Harvest.

Here among the Seasons, watch the Christian
                                    life.
Birth, Marriage, Creation, Death & Resurrection.

See the weeds and leaves turn to rich compost.
Earth to earth, ashes to ashes, dust to dust.
Renew the coming generation!
Conserve, recycle and abandon waste.
The world is wonderful and lives forever if the
grass is green.

Having hung The Four Seasons in our
Parish Church the ladies of the congregation
became enthusiastic and we decided to cover
the ugly plastic red hassocks. So we asked
Kath Johnson ~ a local artist ~ to design for
us and we all worked away at them. I was
given two very long bell pulls. These we cut,
sewed canvas on the sides and covered this
with plain wine red. These were very effective
and took the minimum time to complete.

After learning how to do diagonal stitch on one of these the ladies & the more experienced needle-women progressed on to more difficult designs. Finally I designed some "church window" foot stools to use the oddments of wool left over and to recover some venerable old horrors of hassocks that most people preferred for kneeling on in comfort.

Florentine is a beautiful stitch and most suitable for beginners as it travels at such a pace, leaping over the canvas and getting a lot done in a short time. So encouraging for the less experienced! Later, we stitchers become addicted to the work and speed in completing it is no longer paramount.

The basic Florentine stitch (which goes back to medieval times) is worked straight up and down over 4 threads. I hope the diagrams make this clear. The stitch can be worked equally well from left to right, or right to left. The simplest stitch is worked in three shades or colours and makes a neat little repeat lozenge. We used it for the outsides of the kneelers using up all our oddments of wool. We even found we could vary the colours as we went round the corners.~~

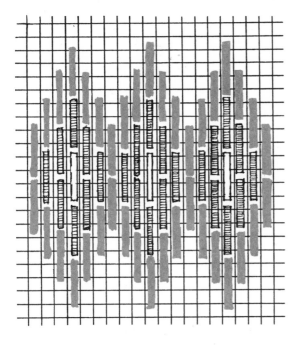

For the long Altar Kneeler we used a more ambitious design. Every one thinks it looks very difficult. But contrari-wise: it is very easy. The apparently diff-erent length of stitch is an optical illusion. All the stitches are made over four threads. It is when they are grouped together that the eye is deceived. I'll draw a coloured diagram to try and make this easy to understand. The design can be worked in several colours but five shades of each colour are needed. The minimum is two basic colours. We used six in five different shades so that thirty shades were embroidered into the canvas. So as to avoid confusion with seven workers

engaged on the long Kneeler I worked one
of the lozenges in each colour to start every~

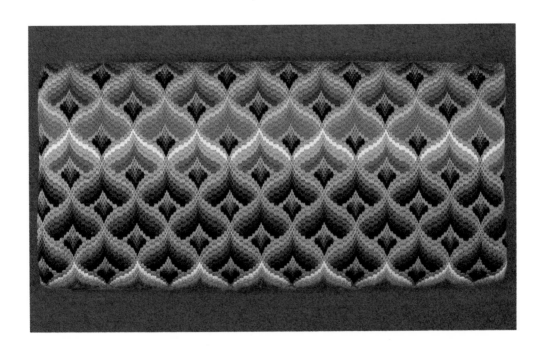

one off.   We took the colours from the rainbow
but in muted shades.   We travelled from yellow
to green, blue, green & back to yellow.   Then
into the stronger oranges and reds. The purple
shade was used as the link colour which re-
peats throughout and makes the smaller
lozenge.   The palest mauve makes the
outer pattern for all the lozenges.
   When I started spreading colour through
the church I chose the colours for the Four
Seasons wall-hanging with fore-thought.
Since then all the colours used in the footstools, altar kneeler, choir stalls, and in
the patchwork carpet have been taken from

the same range.   As a result there is a feeling of harmony.   Originally the long altar kneeler was mounted on two long and one short wooden boxes. A local carpenter made these into seven. This made it easier to divide the work between the seven embroiderers and also the boxes can be shifted up, one each week and the end box returned to the left hand side so that the middle kneeler does not become thread-bare first.   The old carpet we replaced had worn right through on the centre box.

when
these stitches
are crossed
both sides
look
alike

Some needle women prefer working cross stitches on canvas as the work then does not pull out of shape and curves look more curved. It is often helpful to outline curves in cross stitch and then return to diagonal or tent stitch. It is quite in order so to do and it does get over the problem in a symmetrically curved design. I think you can see from this diagram how spiky one side would appear compared with the other. Once the stitches are crossed the design flows instead of 'jerking ~ ~   It was making use

30

of this technique that made it possible for the writing on the paper jacket and the title pages to be legible. The smaller writing can be done over one thread. To keep the work in shape in this case it is best to make the first stitch throughout an entire letter before returning and crossing each one. This gets over a lot of problems. Great searching found the quotation from the Bible. Old samplers always had an improving text as an integral part. I thought I would find something suitable in Proverbs ~ and indeed there is a splendid bit about a virtuous woman, but it wasn't what I was looking for. Eventually working my way back to the beginning through all the "begats" I arrived in the Garden of Eden. That really must be the first recorded reference to needlework ~ or will Chinese and Egyptian scholars disagree?

Most of my embroidery is accompanied by Radio IV or Television. The fighting cocks on the paper jacket just happened to co-incide with the Wimbledon Men's finals. There is quite a pause between points when a few stitches can be put in. ~ Specially if you count the number of times they bounce the ball before throwing it up! I find players are very consistent in this idiosyncrasy ~ I couldn't resist leaving one stitch off the beak of one of the fighting cocks. Of course, he was the runner-up...

Before starting on the altar Kneeler we decided
to make something comfortable for the young
choristers to Kneel on. We had an idea
to depict the story of Noah's Ark. Kath
Johnson designed for us. By working fourteen pieces
and then joining two sevens plenty of us were able
to help. The choir stalls are twelve foot
long and we did not want the Kneelers to be
cumbersome. The stone floor "weeps" in wet
weather and the Kneelers have to be moved
on to the choir stalls between services. So
we used dunlop pillow 4" deep, 8" wide
and the twelve foot long. The embroidery
was worked on 10 to the inch double
canvas and we divided it into five large
pieces and two short ends for each Kneeler.
   Eventually the separate pieces were joined

together and mounted on to the foam rubber.

On one side the storms are gathering and
all the animals are going into the ark.
Glowering skies and sea serpents threshing
about in the encroaching waters ~ wild
animals coming from the left and domestic
animals from the right. With so many people
working there were bound to be discrepancies,
and I must confess that after joining the
work together I cheated and used felt tips
to bring the design into a pleasing whole.

On the other side the sun is shining.
There sits the ark on dry land, the skies are
blue and all the animals are on the way out.

It was this rainbow that determined the
choice of wools selected for the florentine
kneeler at the altar.

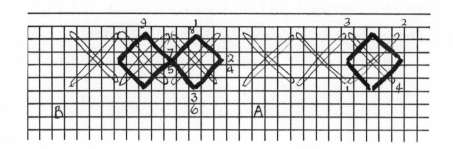

Rice Stitch.   This was a useful filling stitch for some of the small Kneelers.   First a row of cross stitch is worked over squares of 4 threads~ up at 1 (fig. A) down at 2, up at 3, down at 4 and so on.   Then on top using a different colour, or shade the corners are crossed with stitches. Fig. B shows this start by coming up at 1, down at 2, up at 3, down at 4, up at 5, down at 6, up at 7, down at 8 and so on.   Of course in Fig. B 1 and 8, 2 and 4, 3 and 6, 5 and 7 are the same holes.   Rice is a good firm stitch for edges or for lining out a design.

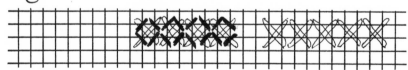

It can be used in a smaller scale as the diagram above shows.
    Another useful stitch for the footstools we found was Scottish.

34

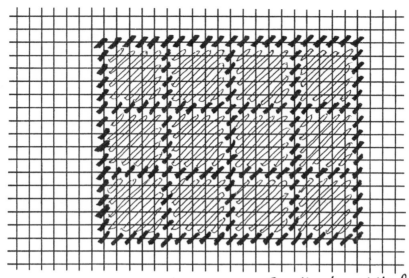

Scottish Stitch.

This is an easy stitch and quite quick to complete. First work the darker trellis in Tent stitch. Then with a contrasting shade or colour work the filling in stitches. I start at the right hand bottom corner and work upwards. The first stitch is another tent stitch — then they get larger to the centre and dwindle down to one tent stitch at the top left hand corner. I hope the diagram is clear.

Another eyesore in our church was the expanse of ugly deal boards, slightly raised which used to have pews on top and an antiquated system of hot water heating below. How to cover this without expense? Like most churches

35

these days funds are low. Then I had a brainwave. In nearly every cupboard under the stairs is a supply of brand new carpet off-cuts. The carpet layer says, as he leaves, "These will come in handy". But of course they seldom do. So what about a patchwork carpet? Every member of the congregation contributed. The carpet pieces arrived in every possible colour. We needed a theme. It was the scarlet pieces that sowed the idea. The poor old scarlet woman! ~ the Ten Command-

ments.   Envy was easy ~ Green.   Soon they fell
into place and a chart was made:

1 "Thou shalt love the Lord, thy God" in blue the colour
of love.

2. "Thou shalt not make to thyself any graven image"
in a chequered design of indeterminate colour.

3 "Thou shalt not take the name of the Lord, thy God, in vain":
a rich brown from: "doing it altogether too brown".

4. "Remember thou keep holy the Sabbath day": turquoise
for rest and serenity.

5. "Honour thy father & thy mother." purple for Honour.

6. "Thou shalt do no murder" in rust chequers for dry blood

7. "Thou shalt not commit adultery": the scarlet sin

8. "Thou shalt not steal" in orange ~ the mixture
of scarlet and yellow both colours of cowardice and/or theft.

9. "Thou shalt not bear false witness": yellow for cowardice.

10. "Thou shalt not covet": green for envy.
The colours leave the centre as beams of pure light
shining from the Christian symbol ~
The BORDER in the colours of the sea for the second
commandment that Christ gave when being heckled
by the Pharisees:
"Thou shalt love thy neighbour as thyself." The sea laps
every shore of our world joining the neighbouring nations
together.

The next thing was to find a method. We used thick cardboard templates 6" square to cut out the carpet pieces. Many of us cut these out and sealed the edges with a little copydex. Eventually these were assembled into pleasing patterns and glued with copydex onto underfelt and weighted down so that the whole was united. The embroidered cross in the centre gave a focal point. It was worked on canvas and some metal threads included to catch the light. Our church tends to be dark.

We were given hessian pieces by the local upholstery shop. These were machined together and used as a lining. The day came when all was ready. It was very heavy. My house is about 500 yards from the church. About a dozen of us rolled it up and then shouldering it we walked down the hill looking a bit like a giant caterpillar! Final stitches had to be sewn when we had trimmed it "in situ" exactly to fit the space. Then the lining was sewn to the edges, large press fasteners were stitched on and their counterparts screwed into the wood and there we were with an exciting splash of colour instead of gloomy floorboards. If other churches would like to have more details we will gladly help.

Just down the hill nearer by a quarter of a mile to the sea is the old church of St. Boniface. Rebuilt in 1070 it says on the notice board. It is a beautiful old church ~ completely simple and the atmosphere is holy.

One of our churchwardens thought that the ladies would like to work an altar kneeler. At the time ancient hassocks in which moth dwelt and mice nested were moved to the rail on the rare occasions when we met there for communion.

It always amazes me how people wonder what we do with ourselves on the long Winter evenings! Anyway, docile as usual, we buckled to and said we would do it. First there had to be a coffee morning to raise some funds. I always insist that only the best quality materials can be used. It's not a bit of good doing hours of work on indifferent stuff and with ersatz thread.

Then "they" asked me to design the long kneeler. I agreed and then walked down the cliff one sunny morning hoping for an inspiration. As usual the atmosphere was serene. What colour should we use? Something very gentle to go with those venerable stones. Moss was growing

40

in the stones around the altar and this patch of green was flecked with golden shafts of sun. Here was our colour scheme: moss green and gold. Next to "see" a design. When I am asked to create I always like to wait until I can imagine the finished work in position. Once "seen" it is much easier to make a success of any project. At home I had all my mother's books on embroidery. She was a squirrel and hoarded everything. Poring through these papers I came across a William Morris wall hanging which I thought could be adapted successfully. This was sketched out onto three pieces which would flow into each other so that three workers could take part in the project. Appletons wools were chosen. With their swatch of patterns it was possible to lay these against the moss. Three shades of green and three shades of gold were used. When first I began designing my own tapestries (you see it is difficult to avoid that word) I found that if the design were brushed on to a piece of cartridge paper the right size with Indian ink it was possible to place the canvas on top and discern the design through the holes. Then with a sable brush and waterproof ink the design can be brushed

accurately on to the canvas. Some people prefer
to use a waterproof felt tip. Either will do.
Later colour can be added. Acryllic or emulsion
paints are best for this purpose. With three people
working on one project quite a lot of detail is best
put in if the finished work is to have any uniform-
ity. When we had all finished our piece we
found one of them was quite out of shape. When
this happens I dunk all three pieces in cold
water and then, having squeezed as much
water as possible out, I roll them up tightly
in an enormous bath towel and tread all over
the resultant roll. Then the work can be
manhandled into shape, pinned on to a
wooden floor with tin tacks and be left to dry;
when it will be found to be straight. It was
necessary to dunk all three pieces in case any
shrinkage occurred. This is why waterproof ink or felt tip must be used. Before
I found this out I had one sad disaster ~~
    A local carpenter made the slightly
sloping boxes and the work was mounted.
The slack was taken over out of sight and
tacked down. The sides ~ very small and not
visible once in position~ were upholstered
with some oddments of velvet. These were
pinned neatly on to the edges of the canvas
and then sewn into position with match~

ing thread on to the wooden box.

For this sort of work I like to use Streetley stitch ~ a stitch used by glove makers. The needle is put in straight through the join. Then a second stitch is put in on top of the first stitch and then the needle travels a short distance diagonally to the next double stitch, and so on.

Streetley stitch. Each upright stitch is made twice into the same holes which the sketch cannot show.

The last thing I embroidered on canvas that I had not designed myself was a charming Parisian griffin purchased from Heinz Edgar Kiewe at his needlework shop in Oxford. As usual, I interfered a little with the suggested colour scheme. Also I wanted the finished piece to be used as a wall hanging. This made it imperative for it to hang straight. I wondered what stitch I could use? At that time I was using tent stitch and had yet to learn about diagonal stitch. So I thought if I did tent stitch the usual way and then alternate rows as if in a mirror that any distortion would be balanced. It worked! I thought I had invented a new stitch. Then I found out it was called Knitting stitch!

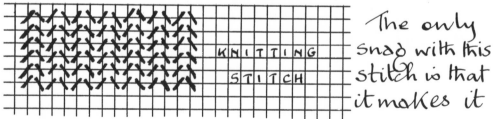

KNITTING STITCH

The only snag with this stitch is that it makes it difficult to jump about on the canvas. The way to overcome this is to do a plain row across the top and then this can be referred to.

When I had finished Griffin with a cross stitch
border and the little fringe had been made using
equally cut threads and a crochet hook into the
bottom row the hanging was backed with curtain
lining and hung on a brass rod. The end pieces
were bought from the ironmonger and the blue
and red cords twisted together. The tassels were
made from oddments of wool left over.

This was the time we
moved into our cottage
and re-named it Yaffles
after the green woodpeckers
whose laughing cry
can be heard in the trees
around us nearly every-
day. I wanted to embroider
something with yaffles
but failed to find anything.
Peacocks galore but never
a yaffle. So, with necessity
the mother, I took the
plunge and drew the
yaffles so that I could
work a central panel
for a prie dieu in great
need of re-upholstering.
This was when I found
out about the Indian

45

ink and cartridge paper technique.

A new challenge occurred when I was taken to Chichester to see the Roman Villa. There were many mosaics there but the one that took my breath away was about twenty four foot square, almost perfect, although not far short of two thousand years old, and it seemed to glow. We were allowed to view it from a cat-walk about three foot above the floor. It depicted a boy riding a dolphin. The colours were auburn, gold and a grey black with a warm natural stone colour. I couldn't get it out of my mind. It haunted my thoughts and interfered with my sleep. My husband was alive then and he begged me not to be such a fidget! Then I thought: why not embroider it on canvas and make a carpet? The thought was riveting and contained any loose moment of my waking hours. Now I had decided to do it, sleep no longer eluded me.

The first decision was which scale? With the help of the picture in the guide book I saw that it could be done in thirteen pieces. Then the pattern fell comfortably into nine squares surrounded by four long strips. You will see that the most important section was the central circle showing the boy riding his dolphin. I found I could buy canvas three foot wide (8 holes to the inch double french canvas) and so I purchased ten yards. This was divided into nine pieces. The extra yard was to allow for turnings on the sides which did not have a selvage. It only gave two inches to the eighteen raw edges. It is surprising how much slack turnings can take up. All these edges had to be oversewn. An inch can soon fray away, which would have been a disaster. Later the outer edges were made by cutting a $4\frac{1}{4}$ yard piece in half longtitudinally and a shorter section made into two the same way measuring $3\frac{1}{4}$ yards.

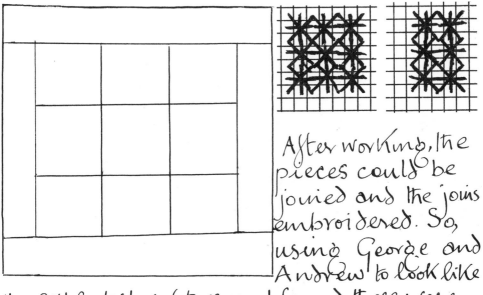

After working, the pieces could be joined and the joins embroidered. So, using George and Andrew to look like the little tiles (tessera I found these were called) I could leave two holes bare on one piece and one hole empty on the adjoining edge.

Then the join would exactly take a row
of George and Andrew. Done this way
the joins really do not show. The sewing of the two raw edges was achieved by
putting them back to back and using Streetley stitch (p.43) and carpet thread. and
sewing into every hole.

I wanted to match my swatch of
Appletons wools against the original
and wrote the curator of the villa. It
turned out to be Margaret Rule. She
was at Chichester before she took
charge of the "Mary Rose". With
her help I descended wearing yacht-
ing soles and laid the colours on the
tessera. Eventually I, too, lay on
the floor to get nearer... I heard a
rustle and looked up. Hundreds of
eyes on the cat-walk were staring
at me! Hurriedly I chose the nearest
colours I could — found all four were
in two or three different shades and
sent off my order for wool to Mrs Mace
and Miss Nairn in their delightful
embroidery shop in Salisbury.
Mrs Mace, sadly, has died but Miss
Nairn still gives the same matchless,
courteous service. I telephone

her and usually the parcel arrives the next day by courtesy of our excellent postal services. People love to grumble at the Post Office but I have only praise for the Isle of Wight service.

I saw that Margaret Rule didn't think much of "tapestry." I questioned her about this and she said she had never seen a "tapestry" mosaic that did it justice. When I began on mine I knew what she meant. The beauty of mosaic is in the flowing lines. These cannot be achieved by geometric jumps up a graph. I started this way and could not get the result I sought. I had visions of the ghost of the Roman stonemason looking over my shoulder and saying: "That b. woman has got it all wrong." ~~ Then I found the answer. Straight rows and squares can be worked in the graph but curves have to be worked freehand over the canvas. Then my carpet, too, looked like a mosaic. This is against all the rules but it works. So, at last it was finished. It took two years and twenty two days and more than three quarter of a million stitches. The outer edge was neatened with the stone coloured wool put in over and over the selvage.

Crewel wool was used throughout. A double thread was doubled into a "tapestry" needle so that four threads went into each tessera four times making sixteen threads in all. The carpet has been down in my sitting room for twelve years. It has seen litters of puppies, wolfhounds (three) standard poodles, four grandchildren, garden boots, friends and relations and shows no wear at all. The hoover cleans it daily and grubby marks have been scrubbed with 1001 carpet fluid.

If you look at the bottom sea horse you will see the geometric scroll work before I cheated and worked freeh and over the canvas. The originator made a deliberate mistake. This was politic as only great Caesar was perfect. He signed his work with a bird in one of the scrolls and playfully I gave this bird a peacock's tail.

Friends who knew my carpet sent me a postcard from Delos depicting a portion of a mosaic there. This, too, I worked ~ it measures four foot six inches by seven foot. Other carpets have been worked in a finer canvas ten stitches to the inch in tent stitch worked diagonally. Having made one offered in a woman's magazine I decided to work my own. It was made in fifteen pieces about fifteen inches by thirteen inches ~ comfortable to work in the hand.

I made a design of roses and rose leaves for the outer edges hoping that this would disguise the joins and distract the eye. The rug tells the story of my family in a cypher of flowers and was

52

given to my daughter Frankie as a wedding present. She lives in the Tropics and you will see how it has faded compared with the matching rug I made for my son John who lives in the gentler light of Bondicut.

This lead to a friend asking me to design a rug for her to work. This was a pleasant job. The first thing is to sit in the room and "see" the finished rug. Colours must be chosen to go with the setting. The bedroom had a charming small design wallpaper of little birds and the carpet was a deep green/blue. There was a lot of white and I thought it would be pleasant to make a chequered pattern of white flowers and a repeating square taken from the little birds. I drew the flowers on separate sheets of paper and put the very few colours in ~ greys and gold with the white. Then the design was brushed on to the canvas in Indian ink ~ just the shape of the petals and leaves and using the paintings as a reference Rosemary White-head worked the panels. These she sent to me as she completed them. I dunked them, stretched them and sewed them together. The outside edges were finished in George and Andrew. When all was sewn together the whole was dunked and stretched and then carpet webbing was sewn round the four sides. Carpet underfelt was then put underneath, cut to fit and the webbing turned back and sewn over this with herring bone stitch using carpet thread.

 Herring bone stitch.

This rug was such a success that Miss White-
head asked me to design another one for her sitting
room. This is a charming room with a wonderful
view of the Thames at the end of her garden. The
wallpaper has an all over pattern based on the leaf
and flower designs of Elizabethan needlework.
Once again we thought we would use the chequered
technique. The rest of the room had pink and blue
overtones. Amongst her antiques was a modern
coffee table with a ceramic top in greens and
blues. These were the green and blue shades
we used for the backgrounds. Then pink flowers
were chosen. These were painted in garlands.
The backgrounds were arranged in five shades
using the darkest colour at the outside working
into the palest at the centre. The outside
edge of George and Andrew was added finally
as a darker shade of the blue range. On the
Elizabethan inspired leaf panels we tried to
get the canvas treatment to look like the
needlework stitches of that type of embroidery.
　　　Both the carpets look well in situ
but we both prefer the one with the white
flowers. In flower arrangements my
favourite is always compositions using white.

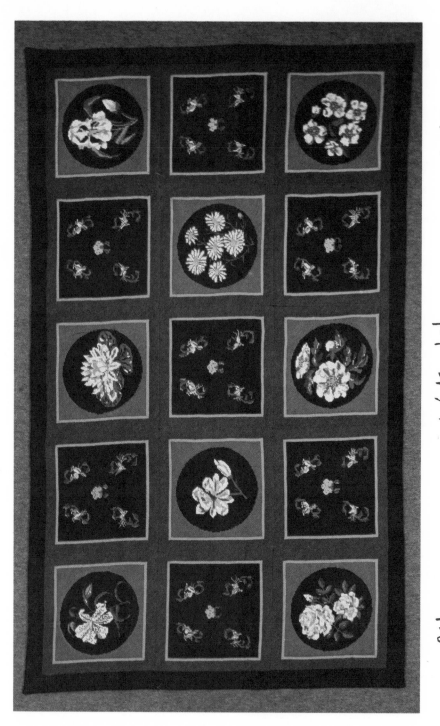

Lily   Magnolia   Water Lily   Daisy   Iris

Rose   Peony   Christmas Rose

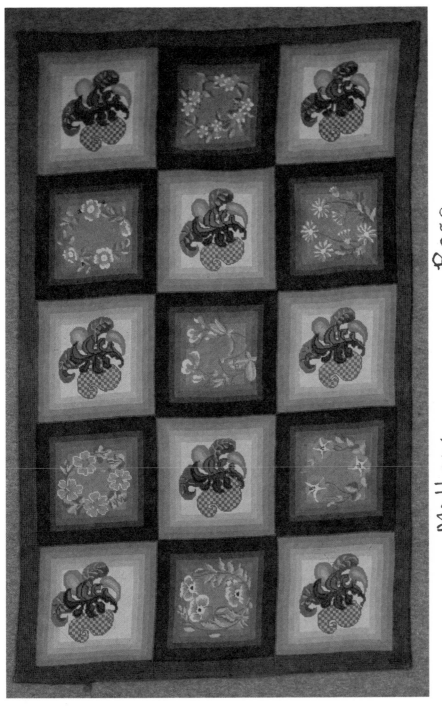

Poppy   Mallow   Pea   Rose   Apple blossom

Convolvulus   Daisy

On the colour pages overleaf are the Delos carpet and some more of the "church window" footstools. Some of the kneelers were worked to cover new dunlop pillow pads. The children love these but older, heavier worshippers prefer the old horrors which, once covered in oddments of velvet or brocade with a canvas embroidered top, may be a bit out of true but are surely more comfortable in use.

The canvas for the dunlop pillow kneelers was cut like this:

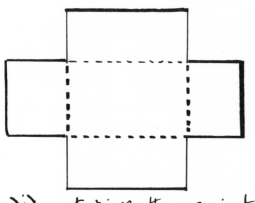

The florentine stitch is very quick to complete round the outside. Most of the actual "church windows" were worked in tent stitch done diagonally. I did not give the saints and angels faces because, unless the needle worker is very skilled, the end product may be a bit of a travesty. The size of stitch makes it very difficult to show fine detail successfully.

Some of us used different stitches. For an experienced worker these are more fun to do and less monotonous. Some of the needlers only like doing the background.

58

These are usually accomplished workers whose eyesight has become tired. Youngsters prefer to tackle lots of pattern - not always successfully, but ambition should never be stemmed. The little rectangles of pure colour are useful for filling in a small space and very good at using up oddments of wool. Now crewel and "tapestry" wools are so expensive not a scrap must be wasted.

The Delos carpet overleaf was, as I said before, worked from a postcard. To get this to the larger size I used the method shown on p. 126. The design was drawn on to large sheets of cartridge paper. It was worked in two pieces - larger than the ones I used for the Chichester carpet. These proved to be cumbersome and I did not enjoy doing the embroidery so much and so it took longer to finish. The year before last I managed to visit Delos and saw the original. My effort wasn't bad considering the small size of the postcard but I did not interpret the lowest row of waves correctly - It should have shown sea horse heads. It was a delight to see the original - although the Greeks do not look after the mosaics and lavish care on them as we do. I think they consider Roman artefacts inferior to their Greek masterpieces! To them the Romans were foreign interlopers!

60

From canvas embroidery let us turn our thoughts
to the ancient craft of

PATCHWORK

which the Americans claim they began. I have
a theory that the pilgrim Mothers took it with them
but no matter. Suffice it to say it goes way back.

My first quilt was made because we had a
Georgian four poster bed and whichever counter-
pane I put on it never looked quite right. Then
I saw a photograph in Country Life of a sim-
ilar bed covered in patchwork and I knew that
this was the answer.

So I chose five basic colours: gold, black,
mandarin red, wine red, & blue/grey. These
colours went with the room. Next I chose a
paper template called long hexagon and covered
six in the six different fabrics ~ i.e. 36 pieces.
Then I played with these as a child plays with
coloured bricks until I had a design which
pleased the eye and then I sewed the pieces
together and repeated the pattern ad infinitum.

The templates ~ which can be bought
from good needlework shops ~ either ready
cut in paper, or metal ones so that you can
cut them yourself ~ are covered with the
material. Cut the cloth a little larger
than the template and tack with long

stitches on the back of the patch.   It is far quicker
to spend an evening cutting out the cloth pieces,
an evening mounting them on the templates
and a third evening sewing them together.

When the last is begun place the patches
to be joined back to back and using good quality
cotton and a fine needle oversew them together
using sixteen stitches to the inch.   Make sure
the needle goes across the join at right angles and
that the thread travels obliquely to make the
next right angle stitch.   When the patches are
opened up the stitch appears at its smallest and
least visible.   If the needle goes in obliquely
the size of the stitch becomes exaggerated and
ugly.   Working this way the work is
completed quickly.   When starting on a
quilt I always have a target of about forty
pieces joined together over three days.   This
makes a fair sized piece of work and once
it starts to grow the progress is stimulating
and not depressing.

When a portion is finished the paper
templates can be untacked and re-used.
Just leave the ones in the outer edges until
they are safely joined to the next section.
It adds to the general strength of the work
if a double stitch is put in at the beginning
and ending of each joining.

Template material

The long hexagon is a pleasant shape
to work with. The shape seems to dic-
tate the pattern that evolves. When I
had my, (pleasing to my eye), pattern
and I had joined them to-gether I was
surprised to find that when I added the second
section of about forty patches that the quilt
had taken over. My centre motif had gone

to the edge and quite another pattern had been born.
There is no doubt that four posters with patchwork
quilts need pelmets to match and it is surprising
how much work goes into the pelmet. In area it
is about the same size as a single quilt, but it
does make the bed look finished and is a "must".

Field of Marguerites Design

I was staying in Devon with my sister-
in-law and she had a pair of patchwork

quilts she had bought locally.   They were in very
gay colours and were based on the hexagon or honey-
comb shape.

Each section was made of six
"petals" of the same material around
a contrasting centre. This was
surrounded with another material
in a contrasting colour of twelve
patches. The design was kept "straight"
by adding two plain patches each side but I
thought it would be more fun to join the flowers
and their surrounds together and let the pattern
flow freely. My copy of those quilts is on page 68.
   I liked the idea of flowers without the outer
addition. At the time the marguerites were
in flower in the fields. Love~in~a~mist was
in bloom on my rockery and yellow doronicum
daisies glowing in the boarders. Here I felt was
a quilt and I called it the field of marguerites.
   The white daisies had yellow velvet centres,
the blue love~in~a~mist green or soft brown
centres and the yellow flowers rich brown satin
or velvet insides.   I made two matching quilts
for twin beds and with a deep blue surround.
I hope they interpret my vision of a meadow
dotted with early Summer flowers.
   It is possible to work out a design on

Template

material

isometric paper.

The simple flower shape

The quilt pattern I met first in Devon

isometric paper.   This can be bought at good stationery shops.

My mother brought home for me from the United States, some time in the forties - just after the war, a box for keeping stockings in. This I find invaluable for patchwork. It is very easy to make one. All you need is a rectangular box about 12" long, 4" wide and about 2" deep.

Then take a strip of corrugated paper $3\frac{3}{4}$" wide and about 30" long and cover it with material. Then fold it so that it makes the little partitions as shown above. Pop this into the box and use it to keep your covered

templates tidy. Using this box the different do
not madden by becoming lost and the work travels
apace.

This is the quilt made in admiration of the
Devonshire design.

Again I made two matching quilts for
twin beds. These cheerful colours look
particularly attractive in a country cottage

with simply coloured emulsion walls and old prints for pictures.

This quilt was made for my daughter Frankie. Again it uses the flower hexagon design but in this case each flower centre is of the same dark purple velvet. There are rows of plain fabric flowers with purple centres interlaced with rows of patterned fabric with the same purple centre. It is the biggest quilt I have ever made and measures 8'6"sq. Unfortunately this quilt went out to Seychelles with Frankie in 1970. I had used a lot of pure silk ~ fortunately because it was lighter in weight than the other material the silk was backed with curtain lining. The silk rotted in the heat and humidity of the idyllic islands three degrees south of the equator. Without the strong lining the quilt would have been in holes.

My reference books on Patchwork are both by Averil Colby ~ published by Batsford. The first one I owned was called: "Patchwork Quilts" and the next purchased later on: "Patchwork." I felt I had lost a friend when I heard of Miss Colby's death this year, although I had never had the pleasure of meeting her.

She wrote that it was a mistake to mix fabrics ~ that cotton should be used with cotton and cotton velvet. In my usual disbelieving way I mixed all the different fabrics together as I liked the richness of the varied textures.

I am still having to spend hours unpicking these mistakes and taking Miss Colby's advice with hindsight!

Frankie's quilt has had to be restored three times and now rests on her bed in the Island ready for her yearly visit. However the purple velvet has stood the test of time. With an unpicking gadget which you can buy for pence from any good needlework

shop, I have removed tatty "flowers" and replaced them with fresh material using the old velvet
centre again. With velvet it is important to see
that the nap lies in the same direction otherwise
it will appear in varying shades. Keeping to
the plain rows and the patterned rows it is
virtually impossible to see where these sub-
stitutions have been made. I do strongly
recommend Miss Colby's books if you are
going to take Patchwork up.
    Also do not start on a quilt. It is
a mammoth task. Try making a cushion
first to see if you enjoy the work. A cushion
can be a wonderful link in a room's colour
scheme. Take the colour of the carpet,
the walls, the loose covers, the curtains,
the furniture and weave them together
into a marriage. Sometimes a pair of
patchwork cushions on twin beds will make a
room come together and look loved.
    I always enjoy making cush-
ions in a harlequin design.
Using six different pieces of
material in two repeating groups
of three deceives the eye and all
of a sudden the pattern which
evolves at the other unconsidered
angle seems to take over.

71

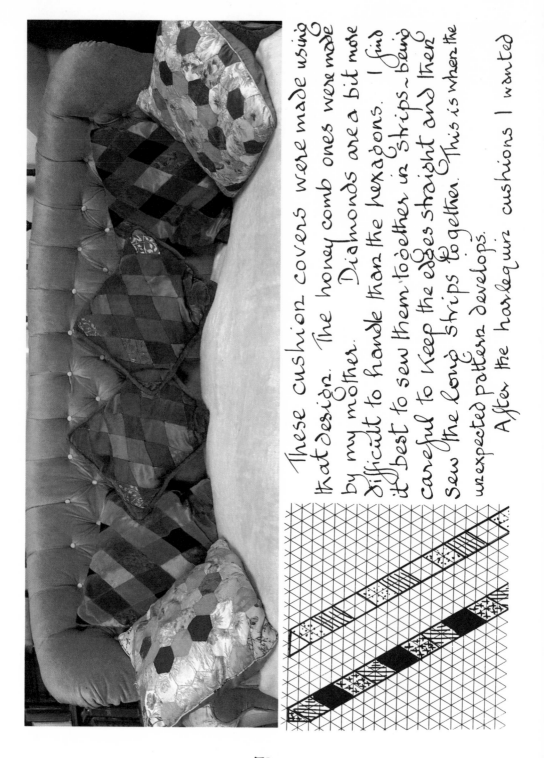

These cushion covers were made using that design. The honey comb ones were made by my mother. Diamonds are a bit more difficult to handle than the hexagons. I find it best to sew them together in strips being careful to keep the edges straight and then sew the long strips together. This is where the unexpected pattern develops.

After the harlequin cushions I wanted

to make a quilt for one of my granddaughters, inspired by the Star of Bethlehem Quilt in Averil
Colby's book. It is dated: late eighteenth century.
So using my usual diamond paper templates, off
I started. But when I began to sew it all together I couldn't understand why I had six points
to my star instead of eight. Then I found out
that there are two different diamonds. The one
on the left makes a six pointed star. The one
on the right an eight pointed one ~ ~ ~

The quilt was
made to fit a
small child's bed
about five foot
long. When
Rebecca moved
into a delightful
four poster made
by her father
it seemed a pity to alter the quilt which was
now too short. Unbleached calico was used
to make the frill and curtains with suitable
patchwork motifs appliqué'd on. The pillow,
however, showed so a pillow case was made
in the same style. The quilt was lined with
already quilted cotton material sold for

making dressing gowns.

The amusing eye-teasing Victorian box pattern is made using the left hand type of diamond.

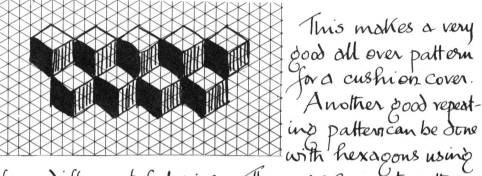

This makes a very good all over pattern for a cushion cover.

Another good repeating pattern can be done with hexagons using four different fabrics. They are sewn together in threes ~ the fourth colour is used separately but the same number of each coloured patch is needed to finish the whole.

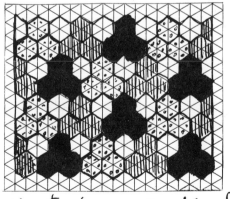

This pattern looks equally well, or even better, done with the long hexagon shown on page 64. All over patterns are always pleasing to my eye. If there is insufficient of one particular fabric it is always possible to use another in the same tone of colour to keep the pattern going

Then my mother sent me a sketch of the pattern
of an ancient Byzantine tesselated pavement
because she thought it would lend itself to a
patchwork.   The templates are hexagons,
squares, triangles and diamonds.   I think
it looks like an early wheel with which they

were having trouble!

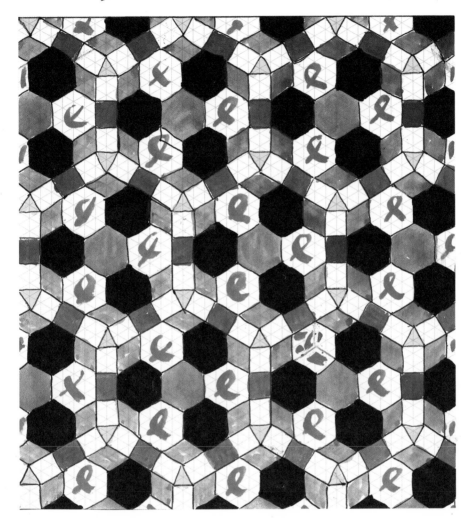

The crude colours have been used in this diagram because, hopefully, it makes it easier to follow. The black has been used because the darkest colour chosen usually dominates the quilt. On the quilt on the left varying "wheels" have been used as part of the whole.

Quite a difference can be made to a design by the size of the patch.   The difference between 2½", 2", 1¼" and 1" hexagons is quite remarkable. Something that I found out the hard way was: it is more economical to buy hexagons and cut the diamonds from them.

It was making the Victorian box pattern that made me aware of this. Of course, if you are using large diamonds this does not work.

Octagons make a change of design but they need small squares to obtain an all over pattern. Also they are reminiscent of the tesselated floors of Victorian and Edwardian conservatories.

The next patchwork undertaken was a repeat of the one on page 68. but this time only silks and the 1" hexagon were used. Because it is all in silks and satins the colours appear to glow and the quilt gives a different "feel".   It is mounted on a cotton lining so that it does not keep on falling off the bed.   Once lined I like to knot the patches here and there. The orthodox quilts were quilted with an interfacing. This makes them very heavy. To knot a quilt work a cross stitch twice into the same holes somewhere consistent with the larger pattern so that it does not look untidy. Use fine strong thread of a matching colour.

For the lining I sometimes use acryllic fleece. This is sold in many colours and washes well. although it is advisable to wash the "fleece" and iron it before making up the quilt as it is apt to shrink.

I find the best way of using this is to cut the lining about 2" all round larger than the patchwork. Bring the lining over and tack it on to the patches mitreing the corners. Then the joins can be neatened by adding a ribbon - preferably jacquard and running a small stitch on either edge. I like the finish that this gives.

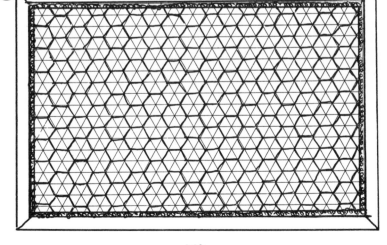

This quilt was mounted before I found out about the acrylic fleece. The quilt and lining were knotted together and then the cotton edging was doubled and attached with small hemming stitches. Naturally the corners were mitred.

John and Rosal-
nd's quilt was
made as a marriage
quilt. It was in-
spired by the XVIII th
century cotton
Coverlet in Averil
Colby's books. The
original is in the
Victoria and
Albert museum.
I did not want
to do the applied
work on the
edges and in-
stead used a
simple sur-
rounding patch-
work pattern.

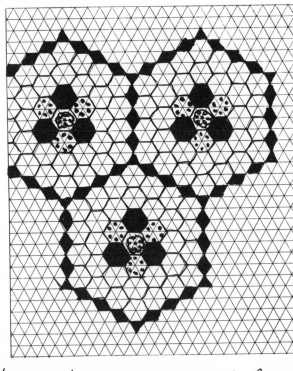

This diagram shows details of the sections of the marriage quilt. The centre section was replaced with a plain piece of material from Rosalind's wedding dress and was embroidered with the initials J and R and the date. The outer edge was made up of a row of diamonds placed long point to long point.

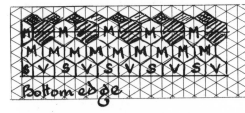

Bottom edge

Key: ⬚ Dark green in a plain & patterned fabric
⬚ Plain shown as criss-cross
M = Dark mauve
S = Red silk
V = Velvet of the same colour.

⬡ Two contrasting patterned fabrics
P = Bright pink.
W = Off white

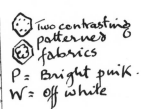

Left hand edge

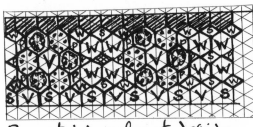

Repeating pelmet design.

Obviously the right hand edge mirrors the left hand.

There is a certain nostalgic charm about the old fashioned eiderdown that graced our beds when I was a child. This often had a central large diamond design with four triangular sections which repeated and mirrored each other. For a change of shape and concept I thought I would try a patchwork making use of this style.

A much larger patch was chosen – the 2" hexagon and velvet surrounded the outer edge of the large diamond. Using velvet with the nap going one way and the other alternately two shades of gold appear to have been used.

The outer triangles were made of the same material as the curtains. These have now been replaced so that the photograph overleaf does not show the original conception. I expect you will think that the triangular sections could have been achieved equally well using four single pieces of fabric. But this was a genuine patchwork and insufficient material was available. The patches were cut from left over material from the curtains as the size of the repeat pattern left some wide strips.

I dislike very much buying material in order to make patchwork. I feel this defeats the whole idea of the craft for, surely, the object of the exercise was to make something beautiful & lasting out of oddments. ~ ~ ~ Of course, these must be new, unworn offcuts.

83

A very pleasant bed cover can be made by
appliqué'ing a large lozenge of patchwork
on to a sheet of unbleached calico. I am
very fond of unbleached calico. Once it
has had a thrash in the washing machine,
hung in the sun to dry and been ironed rather
damp it begins to look more and more like

linen.   It is very strong and it feels and smells
nice.   When we were first married and living in
an African bungalow made of adobe and cocoanut
thatch and the shops had just about nothing to sell
because of the war I made all our curtains of
unbleached calico and applied a strip of coloured shirting, with the stripes running horizontally,
both at the top and at the bottom. The curtains
looked very attractive.   This same technique
was used when I appliqué'd patchwork stars
to Rebecca's four poster curtains shown on page
72.

Only once did I attempt a circular quilt.
Some close friends who were married from
Peacock Vane asked me to make them a quilt
for their circular bed.   (Frankie's quilt on
page 69 was made enormous because I had
a hunch it would land up one day on a circular bed ~ it may still do so.)   At that
time they had yet to buy the bed, but they
wanted a quilt which would envelop a
large divan or hang over a circular bed.
This was the sort of commission I
relish and an entirely new challenge.
I thought of circles growing larger ~
just as the waves which ripple in a pond
if a stone is dropped in.   This idea of
widening ripples meant that there must

be a central motif from which they could
emanate.

To me it always seems easier to conceive a
design if a poem has concentrated thought. So
I sat and brooded and up bubbled:

The Marriage Quilt.

Love is a bright star,
Sometimes obscured by cloud or washed by rain,
Dimmed by the business of everyday
When office and domestic chores delay.

Chained daisies from their simple growing
Like pebbles dropped into a pond
Ripple further than beyond
Forever fleeing
In concentric whorls of being.

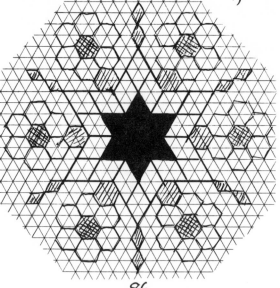

Once the first central star and daisy chain
had been made they were applied to the centre
of the quilt.   Next many daisies were made
in pinks, yellows, whites and blues. Always
as in the marguerite quilt on page 65. I tried
to use suitable velvet or viyella centres. Once
these "daisies" could be offered on to the quilt
they only had to touch on one of their sides
to form a chain.   Once they were applied
the chain theme was assured. Haphazard
patches of green materials were used to play
the part of leaves.
    The butterflies were scattered hither
and yon. Four pieces of fabric makes butterfly. Antenna and bodies can be embroidered
in to add meaning detail.

    Light voiles and filmy materials look
most butterfly like. Spots and eyes can
be added ~ either using embroidery or applique-
ing on little circular spots of bright fabrics.
    The quilt was an enormous challenge
and it was voluminous to work on, but at
last it was finished. In the end I had it

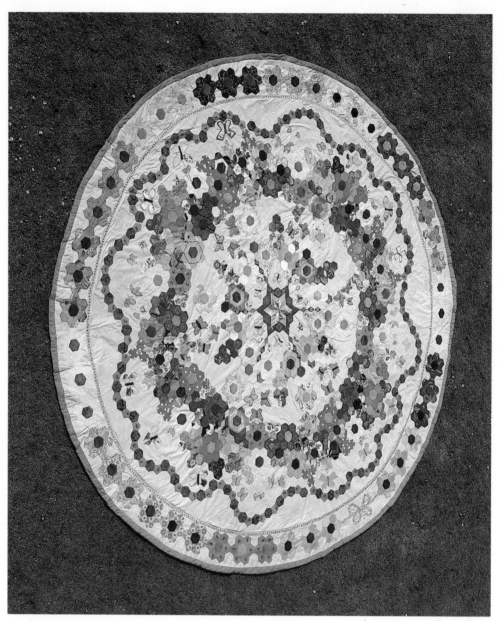

out on the lawn in the sunshine. To my delight
a butterfly fluttered from a nearby buddleia bush
and settled upon one of my "daisies". Although I
said Frankie's quilt was the largest I think that this
one is bigger.

This little quilt was made for Rosie's cot. To go with her name fabrics with rosebuds were chosen. The white patches are of broderie anglaise from the blackberry dress on page 136.

To encourage beginners here are some patches which Venetia, age 12, has prepared. I recommend tacking stitches be put on the back, but no matter. The arrangement shows how they can be joined with triangles & diamonds cut from the hexagons.
see page 78.

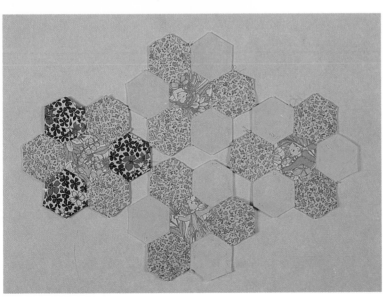

I made some attempts to make patchwork garments ~ but with the exception of Frankie's mini-dress ~ they were not really successful. Patchwork is full of joins, however neatly made, so that it becomes even more bulky when used in conjunction with a dress pattern. It only works if the pattern is of the simplest. Also it must be lined which, again, tends to make it clumsy.

One mistake was using man-made fibre with cotton, satin and velvet. A long A-line skirt made this way was a disaster. The man-made fibre frayed away almost immediately. The offending diamonds were replaced with proper fabric and the skirt became the red and black harlequin cushions shown on page 72. So never use loosely woven artificial silk/satin material of man-made fibre.

Then a bolero proved too bulky and never really set well.

Frankie's mini dress was a success. It was made early in the '70s and still looks as new. You will see that only thin cottons were chosen. It was lined with hand-kerchief cotton and the lining was brought from the back over the raw edges to the front to give a neat finish to the work. The hem edge was garnished with a little cotton lace trimming.

Attractive accessories can be made from patches.
The technique is particularly useful for making
belts. They need to be mounted on a strong inter-
lining material such as vilene or lightweight
tailor's canvas, and then lined with a gripping
material such as vyella. They can be united
with buckle and clasp or with two attractive
buttons and matching button holes.

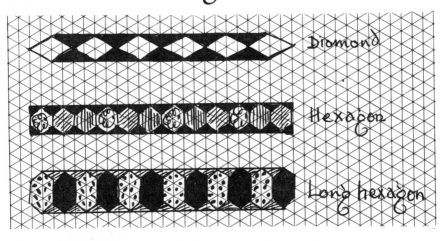

Handbags, also, have proved worthwhile.
Very expensive handles can be bought at good
needlework shops ~ the kind that are sold for
making up petit-point evening handbags.
Patchwork can be successfully mounted on
inexpensive cane handles but these are more
difficult to find. Sometimes a discarded
handbag handle can be re-used. The handle
is covered with material cut on the cross
and then joined to the patches.

The main body was stiffened with a thin buckram.
The sides are soft velvet.   Inside was lined with
silk.   Easy to make and a very useful bag for use
in the evening.

COLLAGE

From simple cross stitch, canvas embroidery, plain sewing used with patches let us turn to the excitement of collage.

There are many forms of collage. Some artists make pictures using cut out pieces of different textured papers and stick them together on a strong backing. I have seen beautiful work done this way. Particularly I admire Oliver Cox's work ~ he is the well known gifted architect.

Then adventurous school teachers cover sections of cardboard with glue and make patterns by pouring on natural things such as sand, split peas, orange lentils and white haricot beans.

For want of a better word, I call needlework pictures, using applied work together with a highlighting of embroidery, collage.

The first thing is to want to do it. Unless you really feel moved to make a collage it rarely comes off. Choose a subject ~ a still-life is very suitable. If you are not a natural artist do not hesitate to crib from someone else. Christmas cards have some superb designs to exploit.

One of the most successful collages I ever made was the Noah's Ark. I did it for my grandchildren. My mother gave me a piece of material about 24" x 36" and it was glittering and sand coloured. It reminded me of the sun shining on the Sahara and that's what started the Noah's Ark off. I drew a picture the same size as I intended the finished collage to be. There was the Ark, Mr and Mrs Noah. Ham, Seth and Japheth. There was a tree in which a pair of owls perched and two monkeys were larking about. As far as the eye could see, out of the distance came a crocodile of animals ~ as they got nearer we could see that they were every living beast in twos ~ male and female so maketh He them. Spanning the whole was the rainbow ~ God's promise that He'd never do it again. It was a very fierce God in the Old Testament.

Once the picture is made then comes the fun of choosing suitable materials. I have boxes of oddments in my studio ready for this purpose. If ever I throw anything away I nearly always regret it later. Richard Sparks who frames my pictures for me cut out the clinker built planks for the Ark from an artificial wood wall covering. The cross pieces were cut from a sheet of cedar wood in a cigar box. The tree was made of cocoanut cloth. This is the sheath which protects the young cocoanut flower. Pearl buttons were used for owl's eyes and elephant's toes. Once the materials have been chosen, trace

the piece of pattern to be tackled on to thin see through paper ~ greaseproof will do ~ and cut it out accurately. Next cut the fabric a little larger ~ just as we do in patchwork ~ and mount the two together either with a touch of glue or tacking threads. I prefer tacking because if later it is necessary to stitch through the glued piece it becomes very hard work.   Where the material has to bend over angles snip the material back to the paper pattern so that it will fold over neatly.

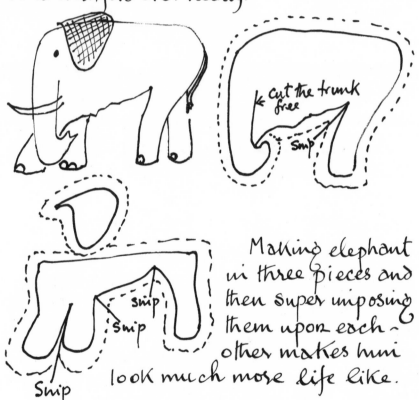

cut the trunk free

snip

snip

snip

snip

Making elephant in three pieces and then super imposing them upon each ~ other makes him look much more life like.

For the tusks ivory satin can be cut on the cross, machined up, turned inside out & if necessary stuffed with a needleful of wool.

As the various animals are roughly ready pin them on to the background. The choice of backcloth makes the collage and it is very important to choose the right piece. If it doesn't please the eye from the beginning it certainly won't at the end.

The rainbow was made of nylon voile superimposing one colour slightly over the next and stitching with herring bone stitch using transparent nylon thread~ very tiresome to use ~~

The mirror, once again cut by Richard, shows the waters encroaching. Although he was mortally ill, it was my husband who pointed out that the ark would throw a reflection, so a portion of silk was cut and glued into place.

As the picture builds up detail can be added with charcoal. That's how the crocodile disappearing into the distance was achieved. Waterproof marking ball point pens are useful for putting in features. Fine detail can be shown with embroidery silks and stitches.

The giraffes were made from felt as this has no raw edges to worry about. The leaves were made of velvet cut as if it were felt and then button hole stitched into position. All the embroidery stitches are shown in detail in the final chapter on traditional embroidery.

The most ambitious collage I ever tackled was the banner of St Boniface. It is 6' x 2' so that the saint is about three quarter scale. My grand-daughter Venetia, who was just about the right height, stood patiently for me while I got Saint Boniface roughed out on to cartridge paper. I had stuck two sheets together with copydex. Bishop Edwin Curtis looked startled when I asked if I might borrow his chasuble and mitre. I wonder what he thought I intended to do with them?

After sketching out the various shapes came the treasure hunt for suitable props. Half the fun of collage is finding unlikely materials and putting them to unorthodox use. Gwen Newnham generously gave me her silk Christmas tree. St Boniface is shown tramping on oak leaves. These were cut out of velvet in varying shades from a swatch of out of date velvet patterns – another gift from a local shop. After pinning the leaves on to the background they were then firmly buttonholed into place. The Saxon shoe was made from soft leather and the "foot" put into a padded sock. The bishop's crozier is a piece of wooden beading from our local D.I.Y shop. To make the ivory crook, which was modelled from a photograph showing Boniface's staff at Fulda where he was the Abbot.   Our artist's materials shop had a new type of modeling clay which was worked into shape and matched to a paper cut out sketch from the photograph.   Henry Cleaver cleverly cut a piece of three-ply the same shape using a fret-saw so that the modelling compound could be glued to it for strength.   Then it was painted ivory and given coat upon coat of a suitable nail varnish until it looked not unlike ivory.

The hands were modelled by 16 year old Mark Curtis-Bennett.   He has promised to bring his grandchildren to see the banner in about fifty years' time!

Next the problem for the material to be used for the hands and face.   Whenever material or papier maché are used for a face and hands the end product is apt to look like a guy or a doll ~ a bit grotesque.   Then came inspiration. Chamois leather.   A washleather was bought from the garage for £4 and the face cut out a little larger than the paper pattern, lightly stuffed with cotton wool and pinned into place.

To keep the background from wrinkling it was pinned to my sitting room curtains and then I could work on it hanging free ~ with the help of small steps.   The hair was made from a leather skin complete with fur and the mitre sewn on top. Then the terrifying job of putting in the features. It was the year we celebrated St Boniface's 1300 anniversary and there was a lot of material to crib from.

No mistakes could be allowed - just a very tentative application with charcoal, ~ then feeling slightly more confident ~ inking the features in with a waterproof marker. The whites of the eyes were added with liquid paper correction fluid. Brown eyes were put in with a felt tip, the red lips and a touch of colour on the cheeks using the same method.

When St. Boniface cut down the sacred druid oak all those centuries ago to save the life of a youth to be sacrificed on the eve of the Spring Solstice, he pointed to a young fir tree saying: Take this as your symbol of Christianity for it is evergreen and points to heaven. So from an English missionary in Germany in the 7th century we had to await the arrival of Prince Aelbert in the 19th century for the Christmas tree to be adopted in England although a Devonshire man had given it being.

Legend says that St. Boniface came to Bonchurch and gave our village his name. He is reputed to have preached to the cave dwellers. I think this must be true.   Otherwise why is Bonchurch mentioned in Domesday Book?   Why is St Boniface Down, the highest point in the Isle of Wight so named?

The circle of light behind St. Boniface is not a halo. It denotes light coming in from the darkness.   The half chasuble was lined with red to show that he was a martyr.   With all the components assembled everything was pinned or tacked into position.   Then they all had to be firmly sewed through into their permanent position.   A little ferrule was crocheted to take the weight of the crozier. St Boniface took six weeks to make working between three and five hours a day on him. He took years to conceive and I was very thankful the day the Rector marched him down the hill and into our church.

The macaws are a jollier subject. They belonged to a farmer friend who lives over the hill. We were all having lunch together when Spring was in the air and the macaws were busy displaying to each other.   A rapid sketch and a lot of cribbing from a bird book produced the pattern. The tree was a piece of fallen bark sterilised in a very low oven for hours.   The other materials were quite straightforward. Simple shapes are remarkably successful in this medium.

105

Birds, I have found, are particularly suited to collage.

The seagull is one of the simplest I ever made and at the same time very effective. Crib their flying shape from a well illustrated bird book ~ enlarge them as shown on page 126 and away you go.

Little beads are useful for eyes and lurex thread (available at knitting shops) laid on to the design and just caught with a tiny stitch every ½" are good for showing the sunshine glinting. (Laid work or couching is shown on page 130). Charcoal pencil shades in feathers and underlines shapes. If this is not emphatic enough a dark grey or black thread can be put in on top using stem stitch (p. 130).

I find it very helpful to assemble the work as far as possible and then prop it on a chair and look at it as you go about your daily chores. Usually, as if by magic, you see what is wrong: what needs to be added and what should be eliminated. All of a sudden in-spiration arrives and the work falls into place and is easy to finish.

Material with glitter woven in is very useful for white birds' wings because it catches the light and makes the subject come alive. Blue velvet makes a beautiful sky. Velvet is difficult to work on because the pile seems to make the material to be applied "walk". Pin firmly, then tack, take out the pins and, finally, sew." This seems to work.

When the collage is finished cut a firm piece of cardboard to the size you wish the picture to be and lightly glue on to it a sheet of cotton wool. Then place the collage on top and turn the picture over.

Now with long threads work from one side to the other.

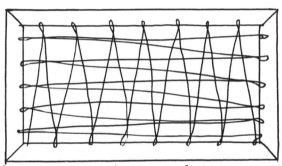

This holds the collage firm and true. Now it can be glued to a slightly larger piece of lightweight hardboard. This should first be covered with material, tinted paper or hessian. I prefer hessian because it can be colour washed with emulsion paint to almost any colour.

My picture framer then puts a box frame around which stands about ½" from the collage and prevents the work becoming squashed.

Seagull's background is of three pieces of material: blue crêpe de chine sky, corn colour linen sand and metal damask and blue/green sea. Bird is one simple shape high lighted with silver couching. Ship & reflection are of three pieces of applied cloth. Rigging was embroidered in stem stitch.

From the Revelation of St. John. Chapter 1   Verses 9~20

Now for something simple. This charming little collage was made at school by my
grand daughter Rebecca when she was eight.
The background is navy blue needlecord. The
ears, face and dress are made of felt "sort of"
buttonholed on. The tail, arms and legs
are in "sort of" chain stitch and the paws
are almost satin stitch. It is delightful,
simplicity itself and should inspire beginners
and children to have a go. Just think of the
yellow chicks on Easter cards and donkeys,
robins and the like that can be found on
Christmas cards — possibilities are endless!

Another simple collage is the one of the Fairy Terns. These fly, making patterns, over the tops of the palm trees in the valley beside Frankie's house in Seychelles. I love to watch them and they became imprinted on my memory.

Chance has a lot to do with creative collage. Friends brought me back some exquisite silk from China. It was the blue of a tropic sky and damask woven with silver bamboo leaves. I made a dress and with the little square left over — and that had to be joined! — thought: this is a perfect tropical sky. But what to put on it? Then I remembered the fairy terns and with the help of a bird book I got the flying shape. The right hand tern is a mirror image of the left hand tern.

The wings and feathers were cut out of translucent material. The bodies were slightly stuffed and then tacked on. The grey shading on the bodies was painted in with poster paint — as was the green shading on the wings. The feathers were outlined with a sharp charcoal put in very lightly. Then gold lurex was used to highlight the wings using couching. The beaks were embroidered in black cotton. Tiny black beads were used for the eyes.

The end product is effective, but it was very simple to do. Simple shapes are best. It is the wise choice of materials that brings out the design.

I keep bags of oddments of material in my studio. These I "file" in colours and textures. They are in the eaves and to hide them there is a curtain around, which squares up this room in the roof with a clerestory to let in the light and a French window to get out on to the topmost part of my cliff garden.

It is amazing what comes in for collage. Bits of old fishing nets, ancient feather hats, buttons, beads and dried grasses.

When bark of trees is used I always bake it in a very, very, slow oven for many hours. Otherwise the eventual glass fronted box frame and our modern centrally heated houses might hatch out all sorts of creepy crawlies and fungi! ~~~

Velvet is very useful. This I cut close and either crochet round, blanket stitch or button hole stitch to prevent it fraying. Then it can be plain hemmed into position. Live leaves can be used as templates with velvet. Pin them together and cut out with sharp scissors. Autumn colours are to be found

in most normal velvet ranges — also many
different shades of green.

Satin will give good contrast if used on
both the right and the wrong side. Sky looks
good in satin but a more delicate effect can be
made by mounting blue voile or georgette over
a matching lining material. Little lace mot-

ifs make amusing clouds. Little machine embroidered posies of flowers from ancient handkerchiefs
look delightful in would be garden scenes. The
possibilities are endless and imagination runs riot!

Jacob's Sheep was the greatest fun to do.

Verna Quinnell has a flock of these unlikely animals which haven't changed since the Old Testament days. She gave me the horns and her first
untidy attempts at spinning. Now she is expert.
The bubbly untidy wool I crocheted into a shape
~ putting in the spots with the natural brown
spinnings.   The ears, tail and back legs are
all Jacob's tweed.   I was given a swatch of
patterns, showing how the two natural colours
could be woven together.   There was a certain
puckish pleasure in depicting the back legs
in "trousers" of the unfortunate creature's own
wool ~~
        The leaves are pittosporum preserved in
glycerine.   Evergreens can be treated in a
2 parts water to 1 part glycerine solution in
the depths of Winter and seem to last forever.   The background of stripes of green
was a happily found remnant in a furnishing department.   The daisies have centres
of Jacob's tweed.
        To get the horns to stay put I took them
down to Richard Sparks who drilled them
top and bottom so that they could be firmly
fixed to the hardboard with a piece of string
and a slip knot. It was worth being a Girl
Guide all those years ago to know how to
do this!

"Jungle" was another fun collage. Here instead of using one background three separate types of material were chosen to try and get the depth of a tropical forest enlivened by a chestnut brown sunlit glade.

To get the materials together, first they were pinned and then herringboned, with quite large stitches, to each other. A piece of furnishing fabric looked a bit like banana bushes and tropical leaves. The enormous flowers were cut out of a swatch of patterns and applied. Elephant, trumpeting, was made in Scotch tweed superimposing the different shapes on top of each other using a light brown thin wool and herringbone. Little real pearl buttons make the toenails and a piece of pink felt the open mouth. The tusks were made the same way as the ones on page 98. Crocodile is of gold damask - the features put in with charcoal and the snake was made the same way as the tusks using a shiny bit of Chinese satin and a red felt double tongue.

The outer mount was painted dark brown to bring out the dappled sunshine of the picture. The odds and ends of flowers and leaves are all cut out of printed material and then applied into place.

"Mowgli" was commissioned after my show at the Ventnor Library. Noah's Ark was on show marked "Not for Sale" because it belongs to my grandchildren. Human nature being what it is the N.F.S pictures always seem to be the most sought after! So I was asked to do Mowgli and the Jungle Book. (Rudyard Kipling).

Having learnt about faces when tackling St. Boniface, Mowgli was cut out of shammy leather and black cotton sewn on for his hair.

The trees were made from the deciduous bark of my eucalyptus tree. A few branches were cut out of the cedar lining in cigar tubes. and the leaves are evergreens treated in glycerine. Various scrap pieces of fur fabric were given me by Joan Baker who makes such beautiful soft toys. Fur fabric was a great help in making Bagheera, the black panther, Baloo, the bear, Akela, the wolf, Shere Khan, the tiger and Tabaqui, the jackal.

Mowgli means: "Little Frog" so a frog was introduced sitting beneath two very English looking mushrooms. The collage is for six year old Emma so Tiger, hiding behind the bamboos, was not given a fierce face. Kaa, the rock python, was made the same way as the snake in "Jungle" and wound around a bamboo. The Council Rock is a flat beach flint glued with Evo Stick to the background. Minni makes the pool in the glade surrounded by rushes. Appleton's crewel wool stuck with Copydex.

Mao the peacock is displaying. and shamelessly I cut up a picture postcard. Collage is a very free art and cheating is to be encouraged.

Again, the background of sky, hills, middle distance and foreground are all different pieces of material. The Bandar hog, the monkey people, were cut out of suede and glued. Their white faces painted with liquid paper correction fluid and tiny beads used for their eyes. Hathi, the wild elephant, was made of grey felt. I hope it is a success.

William is three so he missed out on Granny's efforts and I cannot put him into a shirt embroidered with cherries. He'd love me to do motor cars or sailing dinghies. but I'm not much good at them. So "Dragon" seemed the answer. Making use of glittering materials, glass buttons for talons and a good black and gold gleaming background Dragon was conceived and sewn. The same friends who brought the glorious blue Chinese silk on another occasion brought me a rubbing of an antique tile depicting a dragon. This has inspired many collages. Always I draw quite a new picture and the dragon in a new position.

119

But it is good to have the genuine article as a reference.
You will see one claw remains outside the mount so that
he appears to be pushing himself into the picture.

121

Finally the anagram collage.   This is something I
think I really have invented. I have made a lot of
them but, of course, they were all commissioned and
live far away. They make unusual wedding presents.
However the Magpies I did as a present from me
and so I have been able to borrow it.

A nagram collages are made up from the letters
of the names of a married couple.   In this case
PATRIC and ELIZABETH HOSIER.

I always like a poem to inspire a piece of work,
here is the description of the Magpie collage.

Take Elizabeth, Patric and Hosier.
    What do you find ?
  Crab, hazel, tit and pie:
      Flowers of field
      And birds of sky.
  Add to this the common osier
        and the letter aitch.
      Bind them in a common spell
    Stitch them in and broider well!

Crab apple, hazel catkins, long tailed tits,
magpies and the pussy willow are used in the
design.   Having H left over did not matter as
it starts their surname and is a good shape.   The
catkins are gold velvet applied with loosely sewn herring-lbone. The
crab apple flowers are cut from floral fabric and applied with
button hole stitch. The pussy willow is golden velvet hemmed on
and then made fluffy by using double strands of silk in a haphazard
way. The tits were embroidered to show the detail. The pies were
built up in layers as shown for the elephant on page 98.

122

TRADITIONAL
EMBROIDERY

So we come to the crowning art in the embroid-erer's world. It takes longer to do and it must be done for love~ for I doubt if anyone will justify the hours consumed with sufficient money! But it does give the most satisfaction. I often refer to it as "polite needlework". I like to have a piece of work in my hand when I listen to Radio IV or attend to Television and talk with my friends. Arrival at a friend's house with a twelve foot square carpet is hardly politic and I like to have a small polite piece on the go!

The frontispiece was a labour of love. When I changed the name of our cottage from Rock Cottage to Yaffles I needed something to justify the name. First I did the Yaffles chair (page 45). Then friends gave me the beautiful antique firescreen complete with the original French silk which was shabby and stained. So I made the woodpecker design and when it was finished I mounted it on top of the orig-inal silk so that when I'm dead the antique trade will not be able to accuse me of vandalism!

It was done mostly in long and short stitch, stem stitch, French Knots and Satin stitch.

123

I·SAW·A·SHIP·A·SAILING·

after Charles Folkard

This delightful subject comes from Alice
Doglish & Ernest Rhy's: The Land of Nursery
Rhyme illustrated by Charles Folkard. When both

124

my children were marriageable I offered it to the first grand child born in holy wedlock ～～ Then I did "Froggy Would a-wooing go" from the same source and "Rosalind chose that for her first born and when Rebecca arrived she had the ship.

· A · FROG · HE · WOULD · A · WOOING · GO ·

after Charles Folkard

It is easier to crib a design than most people realise. To enlarge a design all you have to do is to make a trellis of squares over the original and then an- other trellis of larger squares over the space you wish to fill. Then all you have to do is to draw in the larger square everything that is in the relatively smaller square. You can buy a gadget from stationery shops to help with this but I have never bothered with it. However, it is probably more accurate ~ ~

This delightful photograph of Christmas roses and Holly was taken by Brian Daglish, my cousin.

The sketch opposite shows the enlarged design ready for working as an embroidery.

The trellis on the left is of half inch squares, that on the right of one inch squares ~ i.e. four times as large. It is more satisfying to conceive your own designs but if this is not one of your talents more beautiful things can often be achieved by using a professional design. Never be put off. Just go ahead.

127

This screen was made, before we moved to
Peacock Vane, in 1954. Before the present
beautiful fire place was put in there was an
Edwardian horror of bloated copper and bright
green thin tiles. So a hide was necessary. The
Screen is worked on a pebble tweed background
using applied pieces of fabric in simple shapes.
The feathers are worked in herringbone loosely
placed and the velvet "eyes" attached with buttonhole stitch.

Front

Back

This beautiful purse was worked by Joan Baker.
Although an accomplished needlewoman, embroidery was something she hadn't tackled before.
The Women's Section of the Royal British
Legion were celebrating their diamond jubilee.
So there was a competition in which sixteen
Island branches took part to make a purse for
the Isle of Wight to present their gift of money
to Her Majesty, The Queen Mother. Joan's
bag was chosen. I did not put in a single stitch
but I did make some suggestions about the colour
scheme and the design. It is a superb
piece of work and should be encouraging for
beginners ~~

Now to the stitches and their time-honoured names

1. This is called LONG and SHORT stitch and is very useful for filling in larger areas, especially if you wish to use shading. By changing to a lighter or a darker shade every second row a charming effect can be achieved. The lower diagram shows the first row. Use a ruler and a waterproof ball point to mark the lines about ⅛" apart. After the first row of a long and a short stitch subsequent rows are all long worked into alternate stitches. The final row goes back to long and short.
2. CHAIN stitch. Single stitches make "Lazy Daisy"

3 STEM stitch. Very useful for boughs and stems using one shaded row close to the next and building on.

4. SATIN stitch. Straight stitches for filling in small shapes. A padded look can be achieved by working the satin stitch over the shape and then sewing a second layer on top at right angles. The very padded flowers on Japanese Kimonos use layer upon layer of satin stitch to get the effect.

5 BLANKET stitch

6 BUTTONHOLE stitch. Much stronger than Blanket stitch in hard wear and tear.

7a HERRINGBONE. This is both easy & effective. Worked loosely it can have its intersections pinned down with tiny stitches.

7b. Worked closely it makes a perfect leaf filler showing a vein down the centre.

7c. Worked haphazardly and then using a contrasting shade and overworking it gives the look of a feathery texture to birds. For this effect it is best to use one strand of crewel wool first and then over sew with stranded cotton.

8. FRENCH KNOTS. These are invaluable for working the stamens of flowers. Wrap the silk three times around the needle. Then take the thread from the eye end of the needle and wrap it the other way. Put the point back very near to the place it came up, pull the knot up and sew through into place. A little

tricky to explain but quite easy to do after a bit of practice.

9. FEATHER stitch, which is really an open type of chain stitch working from side to side of the central pattern.

10. COUCHING is the securing of a heavier laid thread by sewing little stitches over it about ⅓" apart. Rows of this stitch placed side by side can be built up into broad bands of colour: particularly useful for metal thread.

Texture and colour are the tools of our trade. By using different shades of colour and choosing textured stitches great depth can be given to embroidery. Don't be afraid to experiment, but start small; when you are satisfied with the result, the time has come to tackle something more ambitious.

This napkin was made with long and short stitch, stem stitch and French Knots from a hibiscus flower growing in Frankie's garden in the Seychelles. I did four different flowers sitting in the sunshine there and the napkins are in daily use.

A paradox I have discovered when trying to paint white flowers is that the more they are shaded with grey the whiter they look. This whiteness can be achieved with either grey or very pale green shading, or a mixture of both. Blue, too, can be used in this way. Look at a living white flower and you will see how very little of the petal is gleaming white. Long and short stitch is best for waxy petals. The side the light comes from should be the whitest and the other side the most deeply shaded. Often a pale green is present in the centre of white flowers ~ especially in bell shaped florets as in the campanula family. If a dark fabric is chosen for the background it makes it easier than trying to paint white flowers on white paper ~ ~

Chose two shades of very pale and not quite so pale grey, a soft greeny grey and a pure white together with off-white or cream. If you shade the picture on page 127 with pencil, fine strokes of black biro and a little pale green crayon you will soon see where the stitches should go when you tackle the embroidery. The spherical shape of the holly berries can best be shown by using two shades of red and placing, carefully, the tiny white spot which makes them appear shiny. The outer edges are the darker red - once again the side the light shines on has less darker edge than the obscure side, ~ the white spot should be placed off centre to give reality. Have a look at any spherical shiny object to see how the light catches it. Again the holly berries work well in long and short stitch or in concentric circles of stem stitch.

As my granddaughters grew up I enjoyed making them dresses embellished with embroidery. I was very hard up at that time and there was pleasure in making something that money could not buy. One of my favourite books of reference is: From the Victoria and Albert Museum: 1938 Catalogue of English Domestic Embroidery by John L. Nevinson. The black and white photographs at the back are so useful and are most inspiring.

A square cushion cover in satin of the late XVI Century gave me a lovely shape in which to put the wild strawberries that form the bib of the two strawberry dresses. Alas Venetia and Rebecca have outgrown them but now number three granddaughter Rosie fits them perfectly.

From the bib design a simple
long pattern was devised to
put round the sleeves or
the bottom of the hems.
So that these cotton dresses
could be worn in the Winter,
also, two red vyella dresses
were made — completely
plain which could be worn
underneath as petticoats —
but they had long sleeves for
warmth.

135

136

This stitch shown on page 138 comes from
the Women's Institute in Australia. It is worked
over gingham.   The crosses are made first on
the darkest squares.   Then the thick white
corded cotton is threaded through with a blunt
needle.   For the dress the stitch was exploited onto a fine check and because the scale is so much
smaller looks like lace.

     The gingham table mat is backed with an-

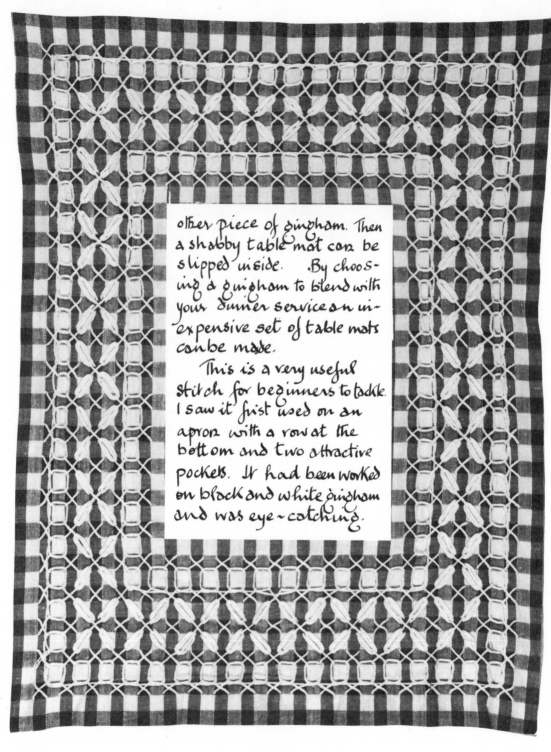

other piece of gingham. Then
a shabby table mat can be
slipped inside. By choos-
ing a gingham to blend with
your dinner service an inexpensive set of table mats
can be made.

This is a very useful
stitch for beginners to tackle.
I saw it first used on an
apron with a row at the
bottom and two attractive
pockets. It had been worked
on black and white gingham
and was eye-catching.

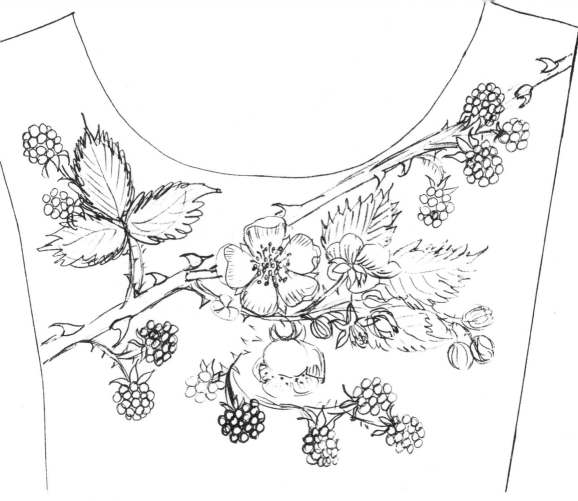

This is the pencil sketch drawn for the
blackberry dress. As a member of the rose
family it has flowers reminiscent of the Tudor
rose. A smaller motif was used for the cap
sleeves. To get the pattern on the fabric pin
it into position and, using a firm table, interleave with
carbon paper for handwriting. After making an impression
in the usual way use a waterproof ball point to trace over
the pale image so that it will not rub away when you
start to embroider.

Here we have Venetia modelling Rosalind's black velvet jacket.   It depicts barley, butterflies and the leaves of the vine.   Worked entirely in laid work or couching, gold, silver and bronze thread was laid with single strands of embroidery cotton.   The thicker thread can be bought in most knitting shops.

Because it was impossible to draw on black velvet the pattern was traced on to thin paper and tacked to the wrong side. Then by placing a needle through the first thicker thread was laid. Eventually when all was finished the loose paper left showing was carefully torn away. Not as difficult as it sounds but not for beginners!

The wild roses were drawn on to the wine coloured corduroy with chalk.   But the daisies
were an experiment.   Having picked some and
arranged them in an egg cup they were embroidered free hand.   This was fun and I do
recommend the more adventurous to try this
method.   It is a bit like arranging flowers
and remarkably satisfying to do.
    I don't think I would have tried had I
not been flummoxed when it came to making
carbon paper show on navy blue! Necessity
really is the mother of invention. ~ ~

141

The backdrop to the patchwork dress and embroidered trousers on page 92 are curtains made in 1948. In those days everything was still rationed and on coupons and our sitting room had a Georgian window devoid of drapes. My mother was in Kenya at the time and she sent me some gentlemen's tropical suiting material in lightweight wool. I think it was called: Palm Beach. Anyway, I wanted a pattern on my curtains and was inspired by the photograph of a Long Cover, early XVIIth century, from my Victoria and Albert Museum handbook.

The motifs separated further apart made a very pleasing pattern. I avoided the blue cornflower because it would have spoiled my colour scheme and though I never hesitate to copy I did feel that something new should be added. So taking the same formula of shape I introduced one medallion of nasturtiums and another of the Mermaid rose.

The curtains have hung for 35 years; first in Twickenham and later in Bonchurch. Now they are on my four poster. People say: "What a lot of work!" But when they last for as long as that and are still giving pleasure surely the effort is worthwhile? The moral of this story is: never, never spend your precious time working with indifferent materials Buy the very best and, with luck, posterity will admire your work.

The crib, overleaf, was made, once again, for my
grandchildren.   I was going to be away in December
for a holiday in Seychelles to be with Frankie, and
I was very aware that I would miss the fun of the build
up to Christmas with the little ones.   What about
making a crib, with all the animals and figures?
They could be wrapped up separately and be un-
done daily throughout Advent, and gradually
build up into the whole joyful story of Christmas.
    First the backdrop had to be painted with poster
paint of the scene around Bethlehem. the angel
talking to the shepherds watching their flocks
by night, the hills, light of a distant watchtower,
olive trees growing on the hill. Lamplit flat
roofed houses around the stable, a path leading
up to the hills and overall the wonder of the
star.
    The stable was a converted cereal packet
fitted into a suitable hole in the backdrop
and, incidentally, making it stand firmly.
It had been painted on thick cardboard.
The crib was made from ice cream sticks
and filled with hay.
    The baby had a shammy leather face with
a bit of pale gold felt for hair and was duly swaddled.
Mary was the most difficult to make. Her
first face made her look like an evil witch!
The third attempt was more successful.

143

Most of the figures were made
of calico stuffed with cotton wool.
A round was cut and then a running thread sewn all round it and
gathered up around a little piece of
cotton wadding — the gathered up
piece used as the neck.

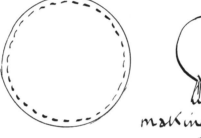

making a head.

This was then embroidered
or marked with coloured biro.
The body was a rectangle sewn
to another one, turned inside
out and stuffed. The head was
introduced into the open end
and the shoulders sewn firmly.
The legs and arms were
single rectangles stitched up
one side and stuffed.
To make the figurine stand
up Joseph was given a staff —
making him, in effect, three
legged; likewise the shep-
herd boy with his crook —

145

made of basket work cane.   The old fashioned
millinery wire, which is covered with silk, and which
I managed to buy from the John Lewis Partnership,
was sewn up and down the legs in the shape of a
hairpin to give more rigidity.

Mary was sewn firmly in a sitting position
on to two miniature bales of hay.   Any thing real
~ hay, straw, twigs, I always sterilise carefully
in a very low oven for a long time ~ to avoid anything hatching inconveniently!

The Kings were made the same way and
sewn securely to their mounts ~ their leg stumps
hidden in convenient boots!
Boots cut this shape from
felt or leather and then stitched
together and on to the legs look
very well and little fingers
cannot pull them off and lose them ~ ~

The animals, with the exception of the lamb,
were all made from the same basic shape.
By choosing different colours and selecting
varied textures it is amazing how distinct
they can look. Obviously donkey had shorter
legs.   He was made of the same tweed as
the elephants on pages 94 and 115, and the
cow of very heavy linen.   Grey horse
was cut out of white felt, black out of
black velvet and the brown from corduroy.

The cow's horns were one piece of cane threaded through and secured.

Lamb was made with pipe cleaners and a certain amount of knobbly wool.

The garments were

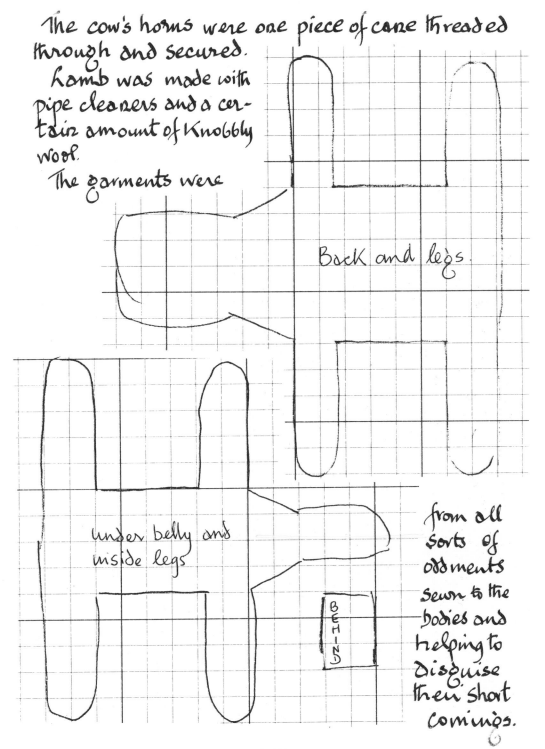

Back and legs.

under belly and inside legs

BEHIND

from all sorts of oddments sewn to the bodies and helping to disguise their short comings.

148

The final piece of work is my most recent and was finished this April 1983.

For St. Boniface Day, 5th June, our Patron Saint, often with the help of the members of the congregation, I try to make a bit of the church look more beautiful. Starting at the back with the wall hanging of The Four Seasons, up through the Patchwork Carpet, 83 Kneelers to the choir stalls and the altar kneeler. St. Boniface's banner and the piano stool were tackled on the way and now, at last, the finishing touch is an embroidered altar frontal.

Again, the colour scheme comes from the wools and silks chosen before and many hours were spent sitting in church, sometimes, I regret to say, the mind wandering from the sermon searching to "see" the finished frontal. At last the vision was made clear. A V shaped design to show Christ's victory over the grave and His resurrection, using passion flowers, fruit, grapes and barley as pertinent symbols of His passion and the Last Supper.

Single threads of crewel wool and double strands of cotton were used in long and short stitch, herringbone, satin stitch, stem stitch and laid work with couching. It is hoped that the grape and passion vines appear to be tossing in the wind. The silk portions ~(I am calling stranded mercerised cotton "silk" because it looks like it)~ are catching the sun and the wool portions are in the shade.

The stole was worked entirely in stranded cotton because the wool might have proved to be cumbersome.

Pure cotton damask in an oyster colour, was chosen for the background. It was pre-shrunk, and a good thing, too, because it lost nearly four inches in the washtub!

In case anyone does not know the reason so many church designs include passion flowers here are the symbols:
The ten petals are the disciples. St Peter and Judas are left out because one denied and the other betrayed. The three parts of the female stigma represent the Holy Trinity and the five male anthers are the marks of the five wounds. The beautiful blue corolla depicts the crown of thorns.

Finally, here is a little dress designed for Rebecca's Saint Patrick day birthday. Worked on a warm white fabric with shamrocks and March daffodils it has a Springtime theme. Too small for her now it lives in Wiltshire with a younger cousin. So it is photographed without its current owner. Soon it will belong to Rosie.

Three Tips.

For left handers: Get an experienced needle-worker to show you a new stitch. Then use a mirror to follow what is being done.

Crewel wool has a nap. Feel it between your fingers and make sure when sewing that the wool flows smoothly through the fabric.

Wool, cotton and thread generally will not ravel as you stitch if you get into the habit of twisting the needle anti-clockwise between stitches.

APPENDIX
of designs which have been used for collage.

Flying Swans

Cock-a~doodle~doo!

cloud made of lace

MOORING
STRICTLY PROHIBITED

Cormorants. (Cigar thin cedar wood was used
for the notice and
stanchions.)

155

Geese repelling
invaders ~ ~

Fairy Terns (p.112)

Although I sketched the leaves into my original design, when I looked at the glorious blue satin background damask woven with silver bamboos, I felt this would be much better. So I superimposed more of the bamboo on to the background. This helped to disguise a join.

If time were no object this subject would be ideal for an embroidery when detail can be lovingly put in. But that is work for posterity ~~

157

I am told by my friends who know the Orient so well that the Chinese dragon is a benign creature.

Always it is searching for the pink pearl of wisdom.

That is why it is straining for the jewel just out of reach.

The pearl was very cheap, I am afraid, and its pink hue achieved by one thin coat of pale pink transparent nail varnish ~~

For the scaled effect multi printed silk was chosen with navy blue heavy satin for the dark bits. A lot of gold thread was laid with couching to line the eye & the crest. The talons were embroidered. Most of the pieces were applied with buttonhole stitch. The eye was embroidered with layer upon layer of satin stitch.

Some notes on Noah's Ark:

The effect of the raindrops was achieved by sewing silver lurex in slanting shafts with a tacking stitch. In between the silver tiny glass beads were sewn to simulate raindrops. One or two were glued to the mirror to look like rain splashing into water.

The cranes (birds!) were made of white and metallic cloth and then garnished with white egret's feathers filched from an aunt's discarded hat. Wonderful hats can be found at Jumble Sales~~ Feathers make wonderful flowers, too.

Although I prefer cocoanut cloth for trees, if it is difficult to obtain, don't forget that the deciduous bark of some trees can be pressed into service providing it is sterilised in a very, very low oven.

A final word. Thirty years of needlework would have been of little use without Bill Holden's brilliant photography.

VAW

Yaffles

19th April 1983

abcdefghi

jklmnopqr

stuvwxyz